CONTENTS

	Page		CD track	
	(Lyrics	Music)	(Vocal	Backing)
Christmas Has Started	2	3	1	16
No Room At The Inn	6	7	2	17
Unto Us A Child Is Born	10	11	3	18
The Gift	13	14	4	19
I Don't Believe In Santa Claus	17	18	5	20
Rock Around The Shops	22	23	6	21
Please Don't Buy Me A ...	27	28	7	22
Christmas Calypso	31	32	8	23
Every Christmas	35	36	9	24
Child In A Manger Born	39	40	10	25
Turn Down The Lights	43	44	11	26
Midnight	47	48	12	27
Ding Dong!	52	53	13	28
Sound The Trumpet	55	56	14	29
This Christmas Time	58	59	15	30

© 1994 Out of the Ark Music

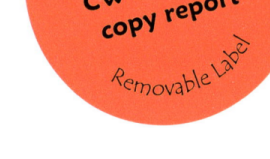

CHRISTMAS HAS STARTED

1. Have you noticed the Christmas trees?
The mistletoe and the holly wreaths?
Coloured lanterns for all to see?
It's so pretty along our street.

CHORUS *Christmas has started,
Presents and parties,
Music and dancing into the night.
Singing and laughter,
Raising the rafters,
Have yourselves a wonderful time!*

2. Have you heard all the Christmas songs?
The choirs and carols, and church ding-dong?
Festive fav'rites from ages gone?
It's so lovely to sing along.

CHORUS

3. Have you tasted the Christmas food?
The deep mince pies and the figgy pud?
Sweet satsumas and chestnuts too,
Turkey dinner for me and you?

CHORUS

4. Have you put on your Christmas hat?
Pulled a cracker, and said "*How's that*?!"?
Played with presents that you've unwrapped,
Or watched the telly and had a nap?!

CHORUS TWICE

Have yourselves a,
Go have yourselves a,
Have yourselves a wonderful time!

© 1994 Out of the Ark Music, Surrey KT12 4RQ
CCLI Song No. 1081292

3. Have you tasted the Christmas food?
The deep mince pies and the figgy pud?
Sweet satsumas and chestnuts too,
Turkey dinner for me and you?

CHORUS

4. Have you put on your Christmas hat?
Pulled a cracker and said "How's that?!"?
Played with presents that you've unwrapped,
Or watched the telly and had a nap?!

CHORUS TWICE

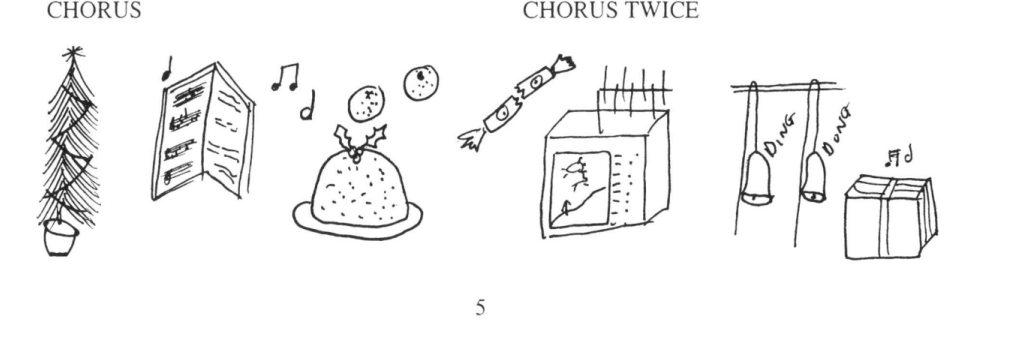

NO ROOM AT THE INN!

1. No room at the inn!
All reservations were made in the spring.
We're full to the brim,
Sorry we can't let you in.

2. No room at the inn!
We're fully booked and the party's in swing.
Please, pardon the din!
Sorry we can't let you in.

CHORUS *Mary, Joseph, tell me what you're gonna do?
There is, no way, you'll be getting bed and breakfast for two!*

3. No room at the inn!
I'd say your chances are probably slim.
We've not got a thing,
Sorry we can't let you in.

4. No room at the inn!
Just take a look at the state that you're in!
Say, where have you been?
Sorry we can't let you in.

CHORUS

5. No room at the inn!
Everyone's saying the very same thing.
We'd take anything,
Somebody please let us in.

6. (INSTRUMENTAL)

7. We've room at the inn,
It wouldn't exactly be fit for a King!
Here, give me your things,
Hope you don't mind mucking in!!

© 1994 Out of the Ark Music, Surrey KT12 4RQ
CCLI Song No. 1095439

3. No room at the inn!
   I'd say your chances are probably slim.
   We've not got a thing,
   Sorry we can't let you in.

4. No room at the inn!
   Just take a look at the state that you're in!
   Say, where have you been?
   Sorry we can't let you in.

   CHORUS

5. No room at the inn!
   Everyone's saying the very same thing.
   We'd take anything.
   Somebody please let us in.

6. (Instrumental)

7. We've room at the inn,
   It wouldn't exactly be fit for a King!
   Here, give me your things,
   Hope you don't mind mucking in!!

UNTO US A CHILD IS BORN

CHORUS *Unto us a child is born,*
Unto us a son is given.
He shall reign in all the earth,
He will be called Emmanuel!
(Repeat)

1 Angel voices sing,...Hallelujahs ring,
For today in Bethlehem
The love of God has come to men,
The Saviour of the world is Christ the King!

CHORUS

2 Leave your cares aside,...seek and you will find,
For today in Bethlehem
The love of God has come to men,
The Saviour of the world is Jesus Christ!

CHORUS

3 Come let us adore,...now and evermore,
For today in Bethlehem
The love of God has come to men,
The Saviour of the world is Christ the Lord!

CHORUS ($x1\frac{1}{2}$)

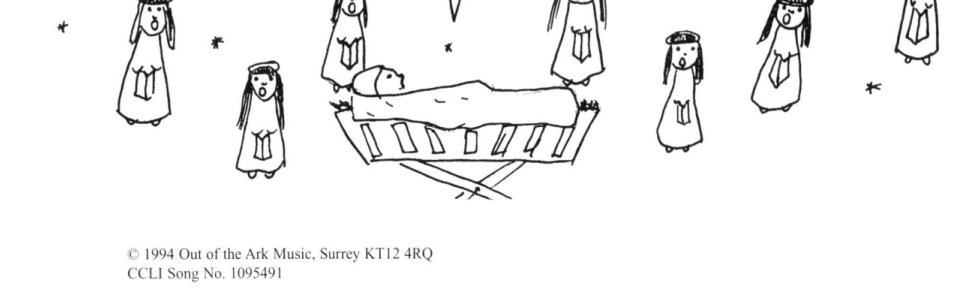

© 1994 Out of the Ark Music, Surrey KT12 4RQ
CCLI Song No. 1095491

THE GIFT

1. Nearly* two thousand years ago,
Under a starlit sky,
Many events were taking place
As the ancients had prophesied

CHORUS   *And a gift was given from heaven to earth,*
The everlasting light.
So let us adore the Saviour born,
Emmanuel, here tonight.

2. Heavenly hosts of angels,
Praising God on high,
Sang of the promised child to come,
The Saviour Jesus Christ.

CHORUS

3. Darkness was over Bethlehem,
Brightly the star did shine,
Showing the way to where he lay
In a manger for all to find.

CHORUS

4. Never before in history,
Had there been such a sign,
For God was born in human form
For the sake of all mankind.

LAST CHORUS
And a gift was given from heaven to earth,
The everlasting light.
So let us adore the Saviour born
Emmanuel here tonight.
So let us adore him, Christ the Lord,
Emmanuel here tonight!

* Substitute "Over" if **preferred**.

© 1994 Out of the Ark Music, Surrey KT12 4RQ
CCLI Song No. 1095453

3. Darkness was over Bethlehem,
   Brightly the star did shine,
   Showing the way to where he lay
   In a manger for all to find

   CHORUS

4. Never before in history,
   Had there been such a sign,
   For God was born in human form
   For the sake of all mankind.

   CHORUS

I DON'T BELIEVE IN SANTA CLAUS !

1. I don't believe in Santa Claus anymore!
   I really don't see why I ought.
   My little sister thinks I'm being so unkind,
   'Cause she loves Father Christmas and I'll never change her mind!

2. I don't believe in Santa Claus anymore!
   Why can't he come to our front door?
   Just think of all the chimney pots he has to climb,
   Well how on earth d'you s'pose he gets the whole job done in time?!

   CHORUS   *I visited his grotto and I got a nasty shock,*
   I stood behind a small boy in the queue.
   When Santa asked him whether he'd been good or not,
   The boy said "No I haven't!" and he pulled his beard right off!

3. I don't believe in Santa Claus anymore!
   I've given it a lot of thought.
   It seems he's in so many places at one time,
   He'll even be appearing in our local pantomime!

4. I don't believe in Santa Claus anymore!
   Why would he hand out gifts galore?
   My mate's convinced that it's his father in disguise,
   But his dad's not that generous so he must be telling lies!

   CHORUS

5. I've hung my stocking on the bed by the wall,
   You never know, it might be full.
   And just in case a certain someone happens to drop by
   I've made a little list of all the things I'd like!!

© 1994 Out of the Ark Music, Surrey KT12 4RQ
CCLI Song No. 1095415

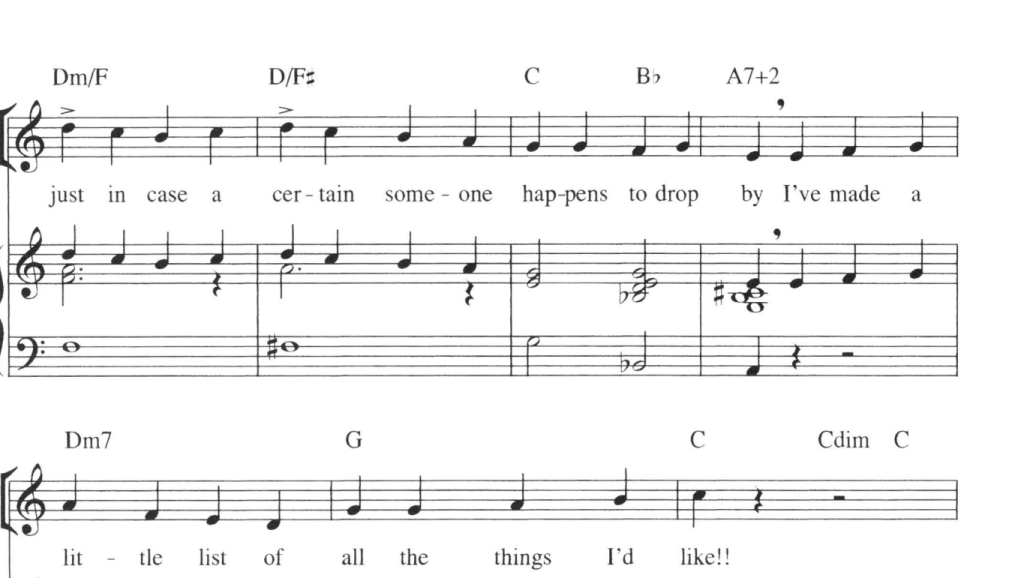

3. I don't believe in Santa Claus anymore!
   I've given it a lot of thought.
   It seems he's in so many places at one time,
   He'll even be appearing in our local pantomime!

4. I don't believe in Santa Claus anymore!
   Why would he hand out gifts galore?
   My mate's convinced that it's his father in disguise,
   But his dad's not that generous, so he must be telling lies!

   CHORUS

5. I've hung my stocking on the bed by the wall,
   You never know, it might be full.
   And just in case a certain someone happens to drop by
   I've made a little list of all the things I'd like!!

ROCK AROUND THE SHOPS

(The Christmas Shopping Song)

1. Come on ev'rybody there's a whole lotta shopping going on!
Gotta get a movin' there's some picking and a choosing to be done!
We're going crazy! We can't be lazy.
It's only days we have left... the rush has begun.

2. Come on ev'rybody there's a whole lotta shopping going on!
Gotta get a movin' there's some picking and a choosing to be done!
They've got the sizes at lovely prices,
I'm gonna buy these today, or they will be gone.

CHORUS *Can't afford to stop, got to pop into a shop before they close. I'm rocking round the shops 'til I drop and it's time to go home.*

3. Come on ev'rybody there's a whole lotta shopping going on!
Gotta get a movin' there's some picking and a choosing to be done!
I've got a bargain for Uncle Marvin
We'll have a laugh when we see him trying it on!

4. Come on ev'rybody there's a whole lotta shopping going on!
Gotta get a movin' there's some picking and a choosing to be done!
I bought some chocolates with lovely soft bits,
There was a box full but now the top layer's gone!

CHORUS

5. Come on ev'rybody there's a whole lotta shopping going on!
Gotta get a movin' there's some picking and a choosing to be done!
I've found a record for Aunty Ethel,
She's rather deaf, but she'll still be jiving along!!

INSTRUMENTAL CHORUS

6. Come on ev'rybody there's a whole lotta shopping going on!
Gotta get a movin' there's some picking and a choosing to be done!
We're going crazy! We can't be lazy.
It's only days we have left... the rush has begun.
(Repeat last two lines)

© 1994 Out of the Ark Music, Surrey KT12 4RQ
CCLI Song No. 1095446

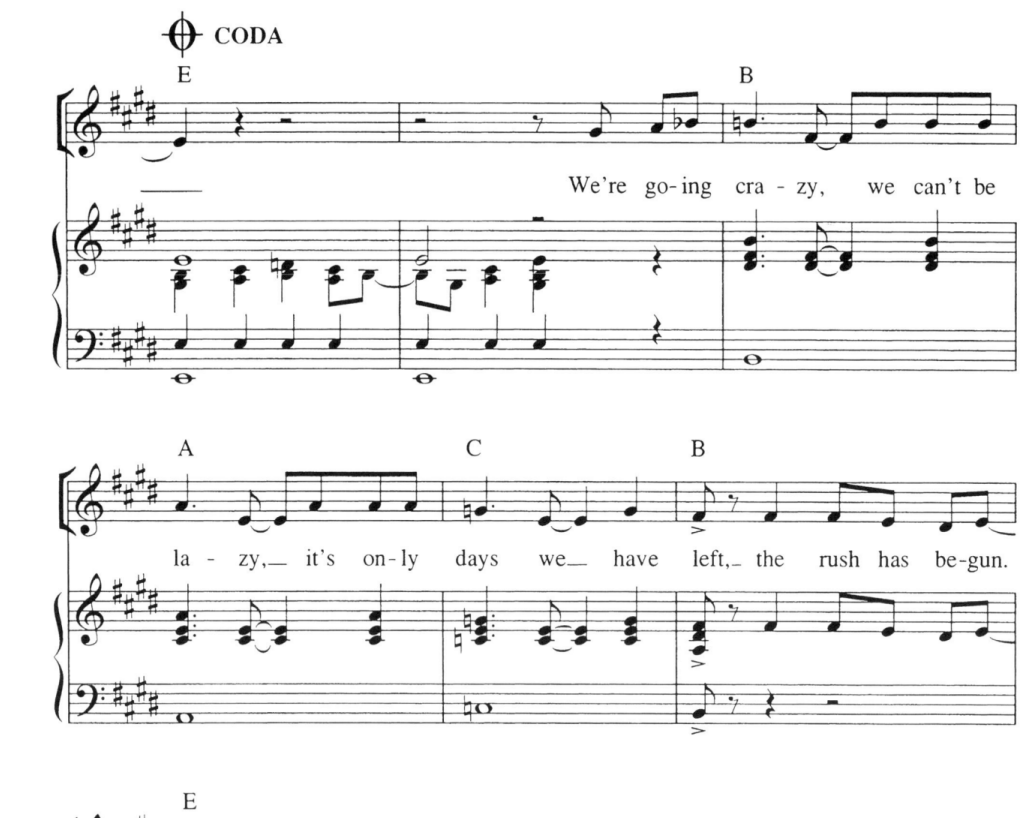

3. I've got a bargain for Uncle Marvin,
   We'll have a laugh when we see him trying it on!

4. I bought some chocolates with lovely soft bits,
   There was a box full, but now the top layer's gone!

5. I've found a record for Aunty Ethel,
   She's rather deaf, but she'll still be jiving along!

INSTRUMENTAL CHORUS

6. We're going crazy, we can't be lazy,
   It's only days we have left, the rush has begun! (Repeat)

PLEASE DON'T BUY ME A .....

1. Please don't buy me a handkerchief,
I've a dozen sets at home.
It would be such a big relief,
'Cause I can't stand blowing my nose! (*Sniff*)

2. Please don't buy me a woolly scarf,
Granny made me one last year.
It would fit any cold giraffe,
But you don't see many round here!

CHORUS *I've got a pile of gifts I've been given before,
Some half-wrapped and put away in a drawer,
It's hard to tell you this, and I value the thought,
But I don't need anymore!*

3. Please don't buy me a stringy vest,
Not unless it's really HUGE!
It would do as a fishing net,
And I'd catch a whopper or two!

4. Please don't buy me a pair of socks,
Even from a posh boutique.
I'm attached to the ones I've got,
'Cause I've had them on for a week!

CHORUS TWICE

© 1994 Out of the Ark Music, Surrey KT12 4RQ
CCLI Song No. 1575203

3. Please don't buy me a stringy vest,
   Not unless it's really HUGE!!
   It would do as a fishing net,
   And I'd catch a whopper or two!

   CHORUS

4. Please don't buy me a pair of socks,
   Even from a posh boutique.
   I'm attached to the ones I've got
   Cause I've had them on for a week!

   CHORUS TWICE

CHRISTMAS CALYPSO

1. Let me tell you a-bout a baby, and his family,
It is written down in the Bible, so you might believe.
Many men had told of his coming, down through history,
Now the time had come for fulfilment of their prophecy.

CHORUS *And they called his name Jesus,
Jesus, the Saviour.
And they called his name Jesus,
Son of the Most High God.*
(Repeat)

2. There was once a young girl called Mary, only in her teens,
She was visited by an angel, sent to Galilee.
And he told her she'd have a baby - how, she couldn't see -
Yet it was her will to obey him, so it was agreed.

CHORUS

3. Well in those days Caesar Augustus issued a decree,
And so Mary went with her husband where they had to be.
There was nowhere else but a stable where they both could sleep,
It was there that she had her baby, born for you and me.

CHORUS

© 1994 Out of the Ark Music, Surrey KT12 4RQ
CCLI Song No. 1095398

EVERY CHRISTMAS

1. Every Christmas we remember
Baby Jesus born to the world.
For this reason each December
Is a special time for us all.

2. Every Christmas we partake in
Fruit and biscuits, pudding and pies.
But when all the food is eaten
There's a message true for all time.

CHORUS *So sing a song - everyone celebrate!
The time has come - this is a special date.*

3. Every Christmas we're all busy
Buying gifts and seasonal cards.
But behind this old tradition
Lies a present come from the past.

4. Every Christmas we have pleasure
Seeing all the glitter and lights.
But there is a brighter treasure
To be found in Jesus Christ.

CHORUS

5. Every Christmas there are parties,
Fun and laughter, music and games.
But the best place we can start is
Finding Jesus once again.

CHORUS

Repeat verse 1

© 1994 Out of the Ark Music, Surrey KT12 4RQ
CCLI Song No. 1095408

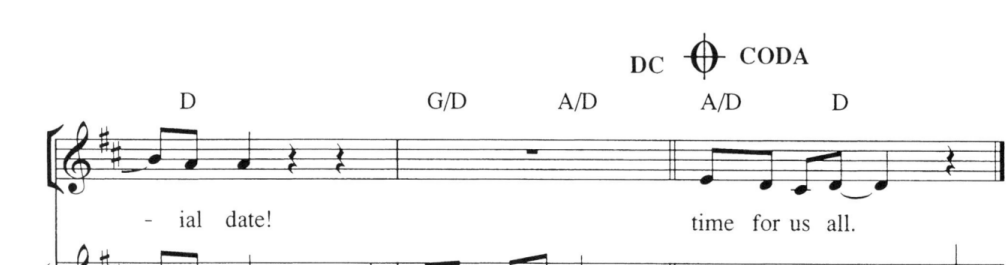

3. Every Christmas we're all busy
   Buying gifts and seasonal cards.
   But behind this old tradition
   Lies a present come from the past.

4. Every Christmas we have pleasure
   Seeing all the glitter and lights.
   But there is a brighter treasure
   To be found in Jesus Christ.

CHORUS

5. Every Christmas there are parties
   Fun and laughter, music and games.
   But the best place we can start is
   Finding Jesus once again.

6. Every Christmas we remember
   Baby Jesus born to the world.
   For this reason each December
   Is a special time for us all!

CHILD IN A MANGER BORN

1. Child in a manger born,
Lies in a cattle stall.
Safely he's sleeping,
Mary is keeping close beside her baby so small.

2. Angels watch over him.
Softly their praises sing.
Voices ascending,
Joy never-ending,
Glory be to Jesus the King!

CHORUS *And God in the heavens above,
Looks down with a heart full of love.*

3. Leaving their flocks behind,
Shepherds have come to find
Jesus the Saviour,
Lord of the Ages,
Here within the stable tonight.

CHORUS

4. Wise men from far and wide
Kneel at the baby's side.
Gazing in wonder,
Praising the Son who
Came to earth to lay down his life.

CHORUS

5. Child in a manger born,
I want to know you more,
Know you are near me,
Love you more dearly,
Jesus, my Lord.

© 1994 Out of the Ark Music, Surrey KT12 4RQ
CCLI Song No. 1095381

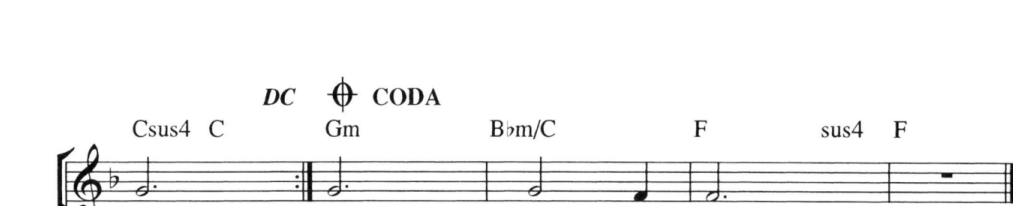

3. Leaving their flocks behind,
   Shepherds have come to find
   Jesus the Saviour,
   Lord of the Ages,
   Here within the stable tonight.

   CHORUS

4. Wise men from far and wide,
   Kneel at the baby's side,
   Gazing in wonder,
   Praising the Son who
   Came to earth to lay down his life.

   CHORUS

5. Child in a manger born,
   I want to know you more,
   Know you are near me,
   Love you more dearly
   Jesus, my Lord.

TURN DOWN THE LIGHTS

1. Turn down the lights and watch the fire glowing,
Colours burn bright and warm.
Now is the time for waiting and knowing,
Christmas will come with the dawn.

2. Dark is the night and gentle the snowing,
Silently white it falls.
Calm is the sight, and soft the wind blowing,
Quietly come Christmas morn.

CHORUS *Night before Christmas - the world is at home,
This day is over and done.
Treasure the moment when everything's still,
Soon Christmas morning will come.*

3. Under the tree the presents lie gleaming,
Ribboned and wrapped and signed.
No-one can see but everyone's dreaming,
Thoughts of the secrets inside.

CHORUS

4. All through the house a slumber is falling,
Settle you down to sleep.
No need to frown, it soon will be morning,
All your surprises will keep.

CHORUS TWICE

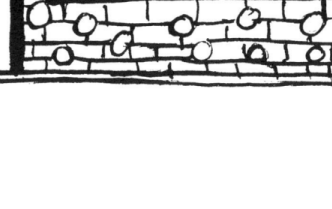

© 1994 Out of the Ark Music, Surrey KT12 4RQ
CCLI Song No. 1095484

3. Under the tree the presents lie gleaming,
   Ribboned and wrapped and signed.
   No-one can see but everyone's dreaming,
   Thoughts of the secrets inside.

   CHORUS

4. All through the house a slumber is falling,
   Settle you down to sleep.
   No need to frown, it soon will be morning,
   All your surprises will keep.

   CHORUS TWICE

MIDNIGHT

1. Midnight - there's the strangest feeling in the air tonight,
There's something going on but I can't make it out,
I wonder what it's all about?

2. Starlight - breaking through the darkness in the dead of night,
Illuminates the path that takes you out of sight,
And all the way to Bethlehem.

CHORUS *Tonight's events were planned in heaven,*
The greatest story ever penned.
Heaven and earth have come together,
And life has come to Bethlehem.

3. Angels - taking care of things that only they can do,
Are waiting in the wings to bring the joyful news,
It's going to turn the world around.

4. Strangers - having made arrangements for a night or two,
Have found accommodation in the crowded rooms.
The house is packed in Bethlehem.

CHORUS

5. Shepherds - minding their own business looking after things,
Are startled by an unexpected happening,
As angel choirs appear to them.

6. Wise men - taking charts and telescopes and compasses,
Investigate the star that takes them travelling,
Until they come to Bethlehem.

CHORUS TWICE

© 1994 Out of the Ark Music, Surrey KT12 4RQ
CCLI Song No. 1095422

3. Angels - taking care of things that only they can do,
   Are waiting in the wings to bring the joyful news,
   It's going to turn the world around.

4. Strangers - having made arrangements for a night or two,
   Have found accommodation in the crowded rooms.
   The house is packed in Bethlehem.

   CHORUS

5. Shepherds - minding their own business looking after things,
   Are startled by an unexpected happening,
   As angel choirs appear to them.

6. Wise men - taking charts and telescopes and compasses,
   Investigate the star that takes them travelling,
   Until they come to Bethlehem.

   CHORUS TWICE

DING DONG!

CHORUS *Ding Dong! (Ding Dong, Ding Dong, Ding Dong!)*
The festive bells now chime.
Ding Dong! (Ding Dong, Ding Dong, Ding Dong!)
To tell it's Christmas time.

1 The angels sing, their anthems ring,
Good news to all mankind!
Ding Dong! (Ding Dong, Ding Dong, Ding Dong!)
Good news to all mankind!

CHORUS

2 Now Christ is born, God's gift to all,
To bring us love divine.
Ding Dong! (Ding Dong, Ding Dong, Ding Dong!)
To bring us love divine.

CHORUS

3 God's only Son, the Holy One,
Is reigning now on high.
Ding Dong! (Ding Dong, Ding Dong, Ding Dong!)
He's reigning now on high.

CHORUS

4 So come along with joyful song,
Let glory fill the sky!
Ding Dong! (Ding Dong, Ding Dong, Ding Dong!)
Let glory fill the sky!

LAST CHORUS *Ding Dong! (Ding Dong, Ding Dong, Ding Dong!)*
....................DING DONG!!

© 1994 Out of the Ark Music, Surrey KT12 4RQ
CCLI Song No. 1575193

3. God's only Son, the Holy One,
Is reigning now on high.
Ding dong! Ding dong! etc,..
Is reigning now on high.

CHORUS

4. So come along with joyful song,
Let glory fill the sky!
Ding dong! Ding dong! etc,..
Let glory fill the sky!

Ding dong! Ding dong! etc...
DING DONG!!

SOUND THE TRUMPET

(Christ Is Born For You)

1. Gather round you people come and
Hear the joyful news.
For today in Bethlehem
A Saviour's born for you.

   CHORUS   *All praise to God the Father!*
   All praise to Christ the Son!
   Who came to earth from heaven
   To show to us the Father's love,
   To show to us his love.

2. Hear the sound of angel voices
Tell the joyful news.
Join with heaven now rejoicing
"Christ is born for you".

   CHORUS

3. Every tribe and every nation
Here is joyful news!
There's forgiveness and salvation,
Christ is born for you.

   CHORUS

4. Sound the trumpet! Sing with gladness!
Spread the joyful news.
Put away your tears and sadness,
Christ is born for you.

   CHORUS TWICE

© 1994 Out of the Ark Music, Surrey KT12 4RQ
CCLI Song No. 1095460

3. Every tribe and every nation
   Here is joyful news!
   There's forgiveness and salvation
   Christ is born for you.

   CHORUS

4. Sound the trumpet! Sing with gladness!
   Spread the joyful news!
   Put away your tears and sadness
   Christ is born for you.

   CHORUS TWICE

THIS CHRISTMAS TIME

1. In a cold stone church, under moon and stars,
   People stand as the organ starts,
   And the candles flicker into the dark, this Christmas time.

2. There's a child awake in her bed upstairs,
   Snuggled up with her teddy bears,
   As she thinks of presents she says her prayers, this Christmas time.

   CHORUS *Merry Christmas to you, Merry Christmas ev'rybody,
   Here's to friends old and new and to this Christmas time.*

3. In a steamy kitchen a mother stands,
   Peeling parsnips and boiling ham,
   How she hopes the dinner will go to plan, this Christmas time.

4. In an empty street under cloudless skies,
   Sits an old man with bundle tied,
   And he huddles down for another night, this Christmas time.

   CHORUS

   *Here's to the message the angels sang,
   Here's to the Saviour who came for all men,
   Born for you and for me, for strangers and friends.*

6. There's a world still needing to hear good news,
   More than presents and Christmas food.
   May you find the love that God has for you, this Christmas time!

   CHORUS TWICE

© 1994 Out of the Ark Music, Surrey KT12 4RQ
CCLI Song No. 1095477

3. In a steamy kitchen a mother stands,
Peeling parsnips and boiling ham,
How she hopes the dinner will go to plan, this Christmas time.

4. In an empty street under cloudless skies,
Sits an old man with bundle tied,
And he huddles down for another night, this Christmas time.

5. There's a world still needing to hear good news,
More than presents and Christmas food,
May you find the love that God has for you, this Christmas time.

Christmas Musicals

By Mark & Helen Johnson

It's a Cracker!

A great new musical that mixes the Christmas dinner festivities with the awe and wonder of the Nativity story. Nine great songs that everyone will love.

* Age: 5-9s
* Cast size: 25 upwards
* Speaking parts: 22
* Duration: c. 40 mins

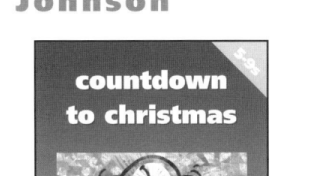

Countdown to Christmas

With the help of a rather unusual Advent calendar, Countdown to Christmas charts the progress of a contemporary family as they battle their way through to the big day. Beautiful songs and a dazzling script ensure that this Christmas musical will be a big hit.

* Age: 5-9s
* Cast size: 27 upwards
* Speaking parts: 27 (can be reduced)
* Duration: c. 45 mins

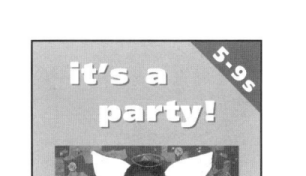

It's a Party!

The invitations were unusual... the guests were unlikely... and the venue was unconventional - but what a party! With 9 new songs, party on and celebrate in style with this brilliant nativity musical!

Age: 5-9s *
Cast size: 24 upwards *
Speaking parts: minimum 16 *
Duration: c. 30 mins *

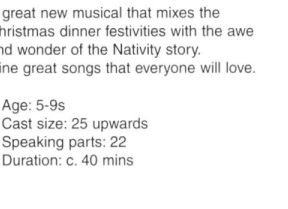

Are We Nearly There Yet...?

Everyone is preparing to make the journey to Bethlehem. Whilst Mary and Joseph, the shepherds and the angels set off, we join the Walker family on their journey.

* Age: 5-9s
* Speaking parts: minumum 18
* Cast size: 18 upwards
* Duration: c. 35 mins

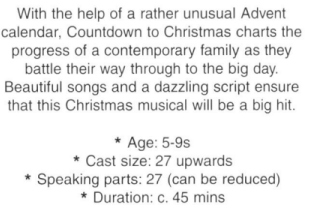

Tinsel and Tea-Towels 🔊

Inc enhanced CD with OHP lyrics, posters, tickets and much, much more!

This true-to-life and genuinely funny Christmas musical gives us a behind-the-scenes look at what happens when children in schools put on a nativity play. Drawing on first-hand conversations with children, this musical helps us reflect on what the nativity story is all about.

* Age: 5-9s
* Cast size: c. 50 (or whole school if you wish!)
* Speaking parts: 5 main & up to 50 with 1 or 2 lines each
* Duration: c. 40 mins

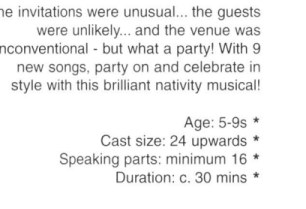

Off to Bethlehem

9 delightful songs present the traditional Christmas story, without the need for lengthy narration or dialogue. Everything you need for a superb production is provided in this comprehensive package.

Age 5-9s *
Cast size: 21 upwards *
Duration: c. 30 mins *

Each songbook package provides:

Quality recordings of all the songs, sung by children – Professionally arranged and produced backing tracks
Piano music with melody, lyrics and guitar chords – Photocopiable lyric sheets

Out of the Ark Music, Sefton House, 2 Molesey Road, Hersham Green, Surrey KT12 4RQ, UK
Telephone +44 (0)1932 232250, Fax +44 (0)1932 703010
Email info@outoftheark.com www.outoftheark.com

songs for EVERY assembly

by Mark and Helen Johnson

The new interactive resource from Out of the Ark Music to get your school singing!

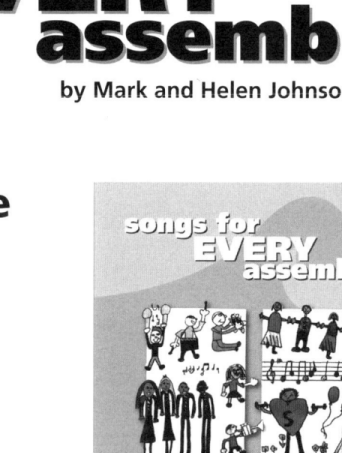

Words on Screen™ is an exciting new way of projecting lyrics from Out of the Ark Music songbooks. The CD ROM can be used to:

- Project the song lyrics onto a screen or whiteboard - ideal for singing in assemblies.

- Synchronise the Words on Screen™ with the music as it plays. Using an interactive whiteboard you are able to repeat or skip verses and the lyrics are highlighted as they are sung. Both vocal and backing tracks are included - ideal for classroom teaching.

Includes all 15 songs from the incredibly popular *songs for EVERY assembly* songbook. Suitable for PC and Macintosh computers.

We've designed two versions of the displayed lyrics - both of which can be used for either the assembly or classroom projection:

The **Yellow Screen** is ideal for younger children or those with reading difficulties. The light background makes the words clear to read and the font used is highly recommended by **Literary Advisors** and **Dyslexia Action**.

The **Blue Screen** has been designed with older children in mind who will be stimulated by the up-to-date and funky layout. Just what you'd expect from Out of the Ark!

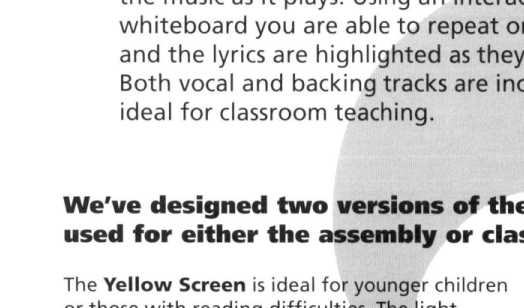

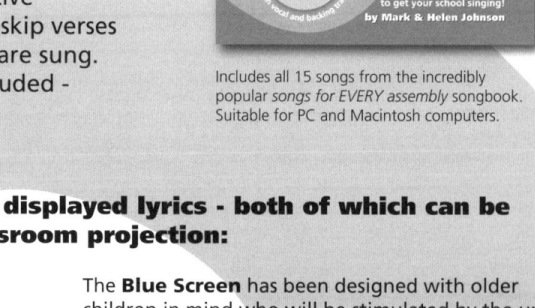